A WORLD OF GODS

ROAR!

NORSE Gods

by Eliza Nodes

BEARPORT PUBLISHING

Roar! Books, an imprint of Bearport Publishing by FlutterBee

Credits
All images are courtesy of Shutterstock.com, unless otherwise stated. Recurring – C_Atta, Macrovector, Anna Timoshenko; Cover, © CC BY-SA 4.0 <https://creativecommons.org/licenses/by-sa/4.0/> via Wikimedia Commons, everst; 4–5, © Anne Mathiasz, Club4traveler; 6–7, public domain, via Wikimedia Commons; 8–9, © Kobus Peche, Yaroslaff; 10–13, public domain via Wikimedia Commons; 14–15, public domain via Wikimedia Commons, GoodStudio, Macrovector; 16–21, public domain via Wikimedia Commons; 22–23, © Morphart Creation; 24–27, public domain via Wikimedia Commons; 28–29, public domain via Wikimedia Commons, ntv; 30–31, © SOPA Images / Contributor/Getty Imageds, Wikimedia Commons, armi1961.

Bearport Publishing Company Product Development Team
Kayla Eggert, Theresa Emminizer, Kim Jones, Allison Juda, Naomi Reich, Steve Scheluchin, Tiana Tran

A Note on Colorization
Some of the historic photos in this book have been colorized to help readers have a more meaningful and rich experience. The color results are not intended to depict actual historical detail.

Library of Congress Cataloging-in-Publication Data is available at www.loc.gov or upon request from the publisher.

ISBN: 979-8-89577-854-8 (hardcover)
ISBN: 979-8-89577-858-6 (paperback)
ISBN: 979-8-89577-862-3 (ebook)

For more information, write to Bearport Publishing, 3500 American Blvd W, Suite 150, Bloomington, MN 55431. Printed in the United States of America.

CONTENTS

THE VIKING AGE

The Viking Age lasted from about 800 to 1100. The Vikings were **seafaring** people who came from parts of Scandinavia. This area includes modern-day Denmark, Norway, and Sweden.

The Vikings worshipped the Norse gods. But we don't know much about how they did this. These people did not write much. Instead, stories were passed down by word of mouth.

The Vikings believed there were nine **realms**. These existed around a huge world tree called Yggdrasil (IG-drah-*sil*). The gods lived in a realm called Asgard.

Historians believe the Vikings worshipped 12 key gods. Each represented a different part of life.

The realm where humans lived was called Midgard.

ODIN

Odin was the leader of the Norse gods. He was the god of war and poetry. He is often shown as an old man with a big beard and only one good eye.

Odin owned two ravens. One was called Huginn, which means thought. The other was Muninn, which means memory.

Odin also had two wolves named Geri and Freki. Geri means greedy, and Freki means very hungry.

Odin rode a horse called Sleipnir (SLIPE-neer). However, this was no ordinary horse. It had eight legs and could gallop through the air and on top of water!

THE SEARCH FOR WISDOM

Odin was always looking for wisdom. He traveled through the nine realms seeking knowledge. One day, this desire cost him his eye.

Odin arrived at a well at the roots of the world tree. Mimir, the wisest being of all, was sitting nearby.

Odin realized that Mimir's wisdom came from the well. Odin asked if he could also drink the water. Mimir agreed, but only if he could have one of Odin's eyes in return.

Greedy for knowledge, Odin accepted. He gave Mimir one of his eyes and drank the water.

THOR

Thor was a very important god to the Vikings. He was the god of thunder, sky, and farming. He is often shown with red hair and a beard. He carries a magical hammer.

The Vikings named a day of the week after this god. Thor's Day eventually became Thursday.

Thor had a **chariot** that was pulled by two goats. Sometimes, he would eat his goats when there was no food. However, he could bring them back to life later.

Thor was the protector of both Asgard and Midgard. The Vikings often prayed to this god when they needed protection or safety.

THE THEFT OF THOR'S HAMMER

One story says that Thor's hammer once went missing. He asked the gods to help him find it. The god Loki flew off to look for the hammer.

Loki found out that the hammer had been stolen by a giant called Thrym. The giant would only give it back if he could marry the goddess Freyja.

But Freyja refused to marry Thrym. So, the gods came up with a plan. They dressed Thor up as Freyja and went to meet Thrym.

Thrym put the hammer in Thor's lap to start the wedding. As soon as this happened, Thor picked up his hammer and took off his disguise. Then, he killed Thrym and all the giants at the wedding!

SKADI

Skadi was the goddess of hunting and skiing. Unlike most of the Norse gods, she was born a giant.

The Norse gods and giants were always fighting. In fact, Skadi's father was killed by some of the gods. However, Skadi went on to marry Njord, the god of the sea. She was then accepted by the gods and became a goddess.

Skadi is often shown wearing skis or snowshoes. Sometimes, she is carrying a bow and arrows and is walking with wolves.

Skadi lived in the realm of the giants. Her home was high up in the mountains at a place called Thrymheim (THRIM-hy-im).

CHOOSING A HUSBAND

After the gods had killed Skadi's father, she wanted to get even. The gods came up with a deal. If Skadi agreed not to harm them, she could choose one of the gods to marry.

However, Skadi had to choose a husband just by seeing his feet.

Skadi was in love with Baldr, the most handsome god. So, she chose the most beautiful pair of feet. However, those feet belonged to Njord!

After getting married, Njord and Skadi tried to live together, but Skadi's home was too cold for Njord. Njord's home was too wet for Skadi. In the end, the couple separated and Skadi returned home alone.

FRIGG

Frigg was the goddess of marriage and family. She was also the chief goddess and married to Odin.

During Norse weddings, couples prayed to Frigg and asked for her blessing. They believed the goddess would protect the **vows** they made to each other.

One of Frigg's powers was that she could see the future. But she rarely told anyone what she saw. Frigg is sometimes shown sitting at a spinning wheel. This is a symbol of her ability to see into the future.

Even today, people sometimes pray to Frigg for a good marriage.

Frigg had two sons named Baldr and Hodr. Baldr was the god of light and peace. Hodr was god of darkness.

TRYING TO SAVE BALDR

Once, Baldr began having dreams about his own death. Frigg was terrified of losing him. So, she came up with a plan.

Frigg traveled to each of the nine realms. She asked every living and non-living thing to promise not to hurt her son. They all promised.

Since nothing could hurt Baldr after these promises were made, the gods had fun throwing weapons at him. None of the weapons hurt Baldr. However, Loki knew that Frigg had forgotten to get a promise from mistletoe.

MISTLETOE

Loki made an arrow from mistletoe wood and gave it to Hodr. The god threw the arrow at his brother. It pierced Baldr in the chest and killed him. The terrible dream had come true!

LOKI

Loki was the god of fire and mischief. He was very clever but dishonest. Loki's parents were giants, but Odin had turned Loki into a god.

It was said that Loki could take many forms. The god appeared as a man and sometimes as a woman. Other times, Loki appeared as an animal.

Loki had many children, including a giant snake and Hel, the goddess of the **underworld**. Loki also gave birth to Sleipnir, Odin's eight-legged horse!

Loki was known as a trickster. Sometimes, he would help other gods. But often, Loki would do things to annoy them.

CUTTING SIF'S HAIR

Sif was Thor's wife. She was a goddess with long, golden hair. One night, Loki cut off her hair while she slept. Thor knew Loki had done it and threatened to kill him.

Loki promised Thor to get Sif new hair. It would be made of gold and grow just like real hair.

Loki set off to see the Sons of Ivaldi. These people were great **blacksmiths** and could make all sorts of things. Loki asked them to craft new hair for Sif.

Sif was delighted with her new hair. It was as good as Loki had promised. Loki's quick thinking allowed him to escape Thor's anger once again!

FREYJA

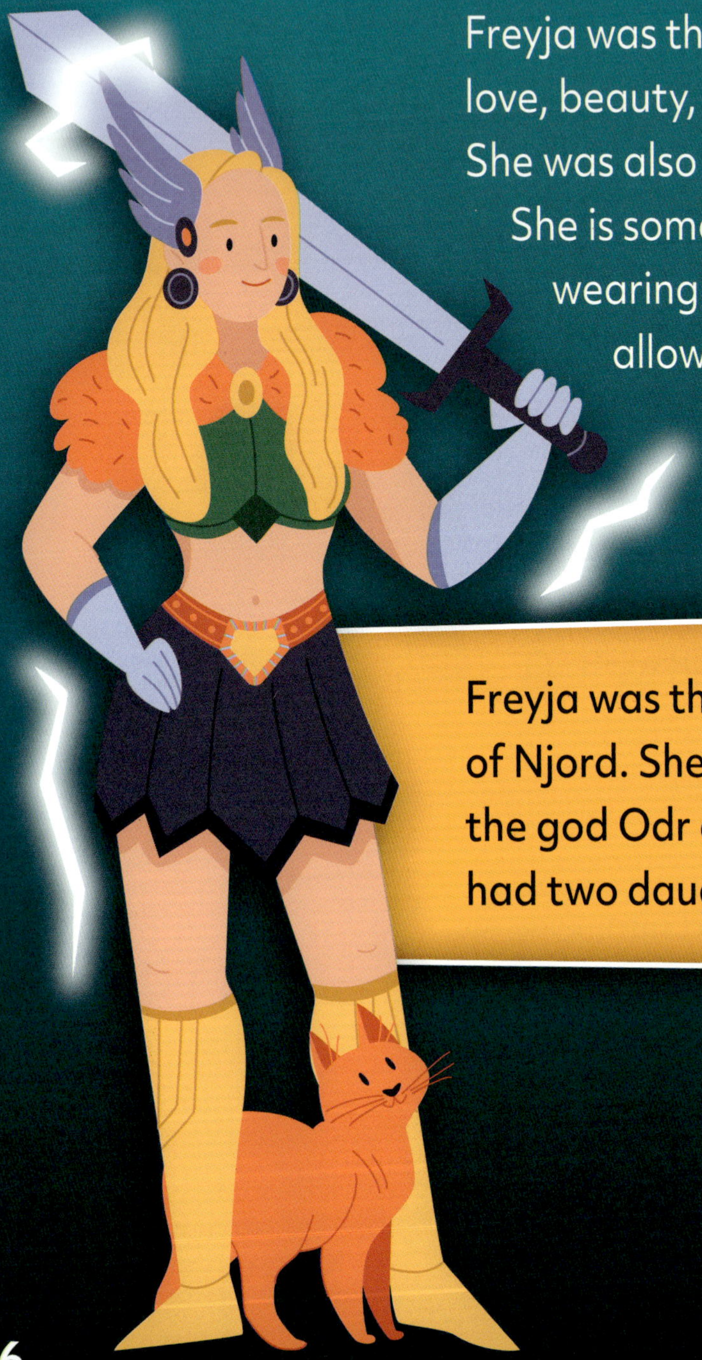

Freyja was the goddess of love, beauty, and **fertility**. She was also a mighty warrior. She is sometimes shown wearing a cloak that allowed her to fly.

Freyja was the daughter of Njord. She married the god Odr and they had two daughters.

Freyja had a chariot pulled by two cats. The cats were symbols of Freyja's connection to the human world. Cats were often kept by the Vikings to protect crops from mice and rats.

Today, places in both Norway and Sweden are named after Freyja.

TEARS OF AMBER AND GOLD

Freyja loved her husband Odr. However, Odr often wanted to travel on his own. One day, he decided to go on an adventure. He left Freyja and their two daughters behind.

Freyja was very upset and began to cry. Her teardrops turned to gold as they landed on the ground.

Time went by and Odr did not return. Freyja thought he might have gotten lost or hurt. She traveled across the nine realms looking for him.

As she traveled, Feyja left a trail of gold teardrops behind her. It is said that the tears that fell in water turned into amber.

THE LEGENDS LIVE ON

The Norse gods were worshipped for hundreds of years. Today, some people still worship them to honor and celebrate their **ancestors**.

GLOSSARY

ancestors people in the same family who lived a long time ago

blacksmiths workers who make things out of metal

chariot a cart pulled by animals that is used for transportation

fertility relating to having babies or the growth of plants

realms different worlds

seafaring using the sea for traveling

underworld the place the Vikings believed they went after they died

vows special promises, usually made when people get married

INDEX

READ MORE

Andrews, Elizabeth. *Norse Mythology (Ancient Mythologies).* Minneapolis: Pop!, 2025.

Dickmann, Nancy. *Stars of Viking Mythology (Stars of Mythology).* New York: Gareth Stevens Publishing, 2026.

Leatherland, Noah. *Life in the Viking Age (Baffling Behavior in the Past).* Minneapolis: Bearport Publishing Company, 2025.

LEARN MORE ONLINE

1. Go to **FactSurfer.com** or scan the QR code below.
2. Enter "**Norse Gods**" into the search box.
3. Click on the cover of this book to see a list of websites.